1993-105

The Threat of GLOBAL WARMING

BY JUDITH WOODBURN

ENVIRONMENT ALERT!

Gareth Stevens Publishing
MILWAUKEE

For a free color catalog describing Gareth Stevens' list of high-quality books, call 1-800-341-3569 (USA) or 1-800-461-9120 (Canada).

Library of Congress Cataloging-in-Publication Data

Woodburn, Judith, 1959-
      The threat of global warming / Judith Woodburn.
         p.   cm. — (Environment alert!)
      Includes bibliographical references and index.
      Summary: Discusses causes of global warming, how it harms the planet, and ways to prevent this worldwide and potentially disastrous problem.
      ISBN 0-8368-0698-0
   1. Global warming—Juvenile literature. [1. Global warming.] I. Title. II. Series.
   QC981.8.G56W66   1991
   363.73'87—dc20   91-50341

Edited, designed, and produced by
Gareth Stevens Publishing
1555 North RiverCenter Drive, Suite 201
Milwaukee, WI 53212, USA

Picture Credits

© Heather Angel, p. 7 (lower), p. 16; © Mark N. Boulton/Bruce Coleman Limited, front cover (inset), title; Sharone Burris, 1991, p. 10; © Mike Busselle/Picture Perfect USA, p. 11; Craig Calsbeck/DeWalt & Associates, 1991, p. 5, pp. 12-13; © Eric Crichton/Bruce Coleman Limited, p. 13; © Gerald Cubitt/Picture Perfect USA, cover; © Mark Edwards/Still Pictures, p. 17 (lower), pp. 22-23; © Chris Fairclough Colour Library, pp. 2-3, p. 24; © Ron Giling/Panos Pictures, pp. 24-25; Matthew Groshek, 1992, pp. 6-7, p. 7 (upper), p. 9, pp. 28-29; © Bill Holden/Picture Perfect USA, pp. 10-11; © Dave and Les Jacobs/Picture Perfect USA, p. 15 (lower); © Jane Legate/ Robert Harding Picture Library, p. 18 (upper); Michael Medynsky/Artisan, 1992, pp. 8-9; Courtesy of NASA, p. 20; © Richard T. Nowitz/Picture Perfect USA, p. 19 (upper); © Picture Perfect USA, p. 15 (upper), p. 17 (upper); © Hans Reinhard/ Bruce Coleman Limited, pp. 20-21; © Gareth Stevens, Inc., 1992, p. 18 (lower); © TROPIX/M & V Birley, p. 19 (lower); © TROPIX/D. Charlwood, p. 21; © TROPIX/ J. Lee, pp. 26-27; UPI/Bettmann, p. 8; © Lee Valkenaar/International Stock, p. 14.

Map information on pp. 6-7, 9 from *Atlas of the Environment*, New York: Prentice Hall Press, 1990, pp. 94-95.

Series editor: Patricia Lantier-Sampon
Series designer: Laurie Shock
Book designer: Sabine Beaupré
Picture researcher: Diane Laska
Research editor: Aldemar Hagen

Printed in the United States of America

1 2 3 4 5 6 7 8 9 98 97 96 95 94 93 92

CONTENTS

The Threat of Global Warming 4
An Uncertain Future 6
Our Planet's Changing Climate............................ 8
Fact File — The Maldives:
   Islands in Danger of Drowning 10
What Is the Greenhouse Effect? 12

Stopping Global Warming 14
Controlling Carbon Dioxide 14
Cutting Back on Methane 16
Clearing the Air of CFCs 18
Fact File —
   The Mysterious Hole in the Sky 20
Bringing Back the Forests....................................22
Turning Down the Heat 26

Research Activities 28
Things You Can Do to Help 30
Places to Write for More Information 30
More Books to Read 30
Glossary 31
Index 32

Words that appear in the glossary are printed in **boldface** type the first time they appear in the text.

THE THREAT OF GLOBAL WARMING

Look up at the sky. The Earth is surrounded by an invisible coat of gases called the **atmosphere**. These gases hold warmth in and keep our planet from getting too cold.

Little by little, however, the atmosphere has been changing. As people burn fuel to drive cars, heat their homes, and run factories, they release more gases into the atmosphere. Many scientists are afraid these gases will hold in too much heat. The Earth could get *too* warm. This is called **global warming**.

At first, global warming might not seem so terrible. Wouldn't it be nice to have summer all the time? But people in many countries are worried that if global warming is not stopped, much of the Earth could get too hot and dry to grow food. Coastal areas could flood if too much polar ice and snow melt. People and animals would die.

Some scientists aren't sure all this will happen. But to make sure that it doesn't, we need to cut back now on the gases that cause global warming. If we wait too long, it may be too late.

The Sun's rays and Earth's gaseous atmosphere work together to keep our planet warm. Some solar rays are reflected by Earth's atmosphere, some by clouds, and others by oceans and land. Those rays that penetrate these layers are absorbed by the Earth's surface.

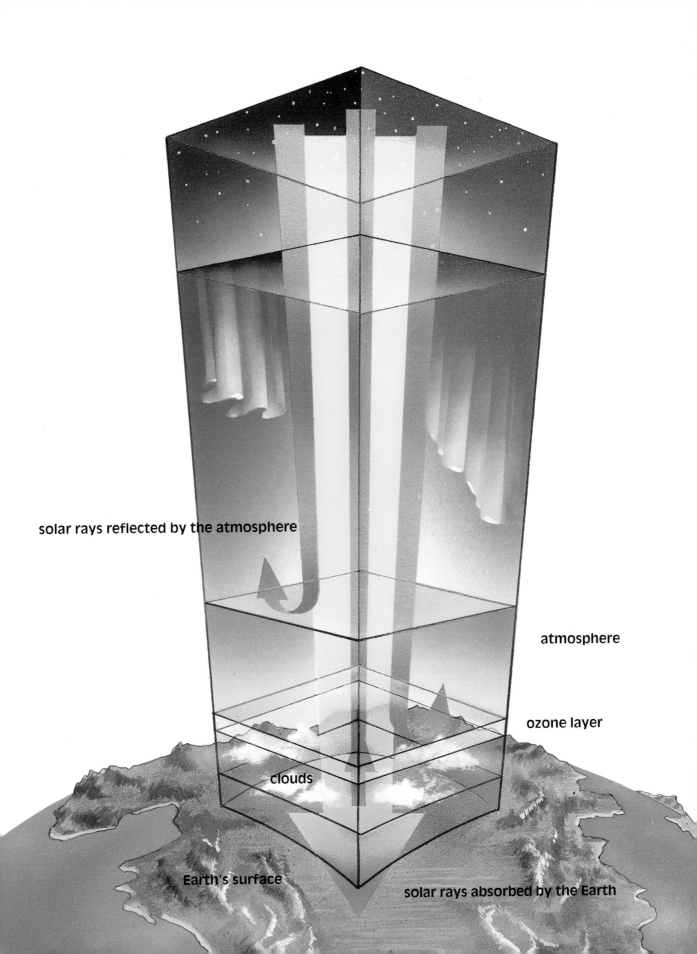

solar rays reflected by the atmosphere

atmosphere

ozone layer

clouds

Earth's surface

solar rays absorbed by the Earth

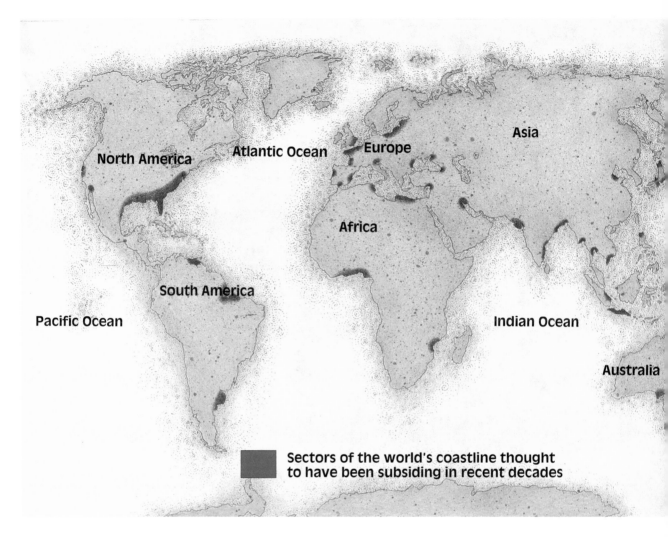

North America

Atlantic Ocean

Europe

Asia

Africa

South America

Pacific Ocean

Indian Ocean

Australia

■ Sectors of the world's coastline thought
to have been subsiding in recent decades

An Uncertain Future

It is hard to predict what might happen if
the Earth gets warmer. Ice covering the
North and South poles could melt, raising
the level of the sea. This could flood all the
coastal regions of the world, where nearly
half the world's population lives. Many
animals living in coastal areas would die, too.
In inland areas, the heat could make fresh-
water lakes and rivers dry up, turning
farmland into deserts.

Above and opposite, above:
Over the next 100 years, water
in the world's seas is expected
to rise by over 3 feet (1 m).
Many coastal areas will be under
water, and rivers will flood
more often.

Opposite, bottom: The flooded
Rio Guayas in Ecuador.

6

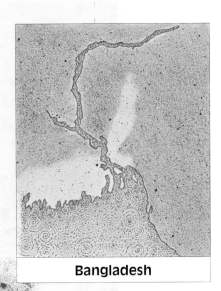

Bangladesh

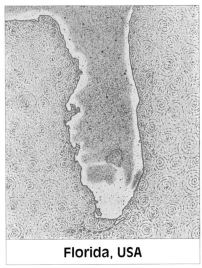

Florida, USA

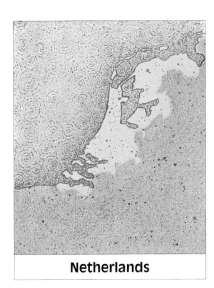

Netherlands

Low-lying coastal areas of predicted flooding

Our Planet's Changing Climate

Temperatures on Earth change with the seasons. They also change over many years' time. About 20,000 years ago, for example, the Earth experienced an ice age, and much of the planet was covered by **glaciers**.

Some scientists believe that human activities are causing Earth's temperatures to rise dangerously high. In the 1980s, world temperatures increased, and the extra heat caused terrible **droughts**. The year 1990 was hotter than any year since scientists first started keeping records in 1850!

If nothing is done, scientists predict that the Earth will warm another five degrees before the year 2100. If this happens, the climate could change more in your own lifetime than it has changed since the last ice age!

Above: The Earth goes through normal cycles of climate change. Each change affects the plants and animals living on our planet. For example, during the age of the mighty dinosaurs, the Earth's climate was hot and humid with lush, tropical greenery.

Opposite, bottom: Some scientists believe that if we do not stop global warming, temperatures could increase by as much as ten degrees in some parts of the world.

The Great Drought of 1988

In the summer of 1988, the midwestern section of the United States experienced a terrible drought. It was so hot and dry that farmers could grow only half of the corn they usually grew. Some scientists thought the drought was our first taste of the potential problems of global warming.

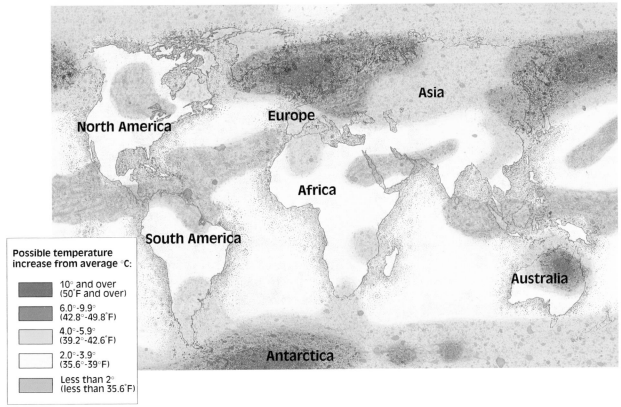

Possible temperature
increase from average °C:

10° and over
(50°F and over)

6.0°-9.9°
(42.8°-49.8°F)

4.0°-5.9°
(39.2°-42.6°F)

2.0°-3.9°
(35.6°-39°F)

Less than 2°
(less than 35.6°F)

North America

Europe

Asia

Africa

South America

Australia

Antarctica

FACT FILE
The Maldives: Islands in Danger of Drowning

The Republic of the Maldives is a country made up of more than 1,000 tiny islands in the Indian Ocean. The people of the Maldives have a good reason to be worried about global warming. Most of the islands are just above sea level, and some scientists say that over the next century, the sea could rise by more than two feet (0.6 m). If that happens, all the islands of the Maldives will be under water!

Some people in the Maldives believe that the sea is already rising. A few years ago, huge waves washed over one of the islands. The waves were higher than anyone living there had ever seen. The water swept away walls and covered almost a whole city.

If the water level rises, the people of the Maldives will have to build special walls to protect their islands from flooding. But the people who live there are poor and cannot afford to build the walls without help. They hope other countries will work together to stop global warming before the Maldive islands drown.

Right: In the Maldive islands, most people live less than 6.5 feet (2 m) above the waves. A breakwater (inset) can slow the waves but will not stop them from washing over the islands during a storm.

What Is the Greenhouse Effect?

The air around the Earth is filled with many gases, including the **oxygen** we breathe. Other gases, such as **carbon dioxide**, serve as a protective covering for our planet. These gases act like the glass on a **greenhouse** roof. They let light through, but trap heat close to the Earth. Scientists call this trapping of heat the **greenhouse effect**, and the heat-trapping gases are called greenhouse gases. Without them, our planet would be at least 60°F (15°C) colder, and many forms of life could not survive.

The atmosphere has only a small amount of carbon dioxide. But a little of this gas goes a long way. Over the past few centuries, **pollution** has increased the total amount of carbon dioxide in the atmosphere by 25 percent. Now, carbon dioxide and other greenhouse gases may be doing their job a little too well.

Right: The Earth's surface absorbs heat from the Sun (red arrows) and radiates some of it back into the atmosphere. If there is too much carbon dioxide from pollution in the atmosphere, not enough heat can escape (green arrows), and our planet will become too hot. This occurrence is the greenhouse effect.

Above: A greenhouse keeps plants at the right temperature.

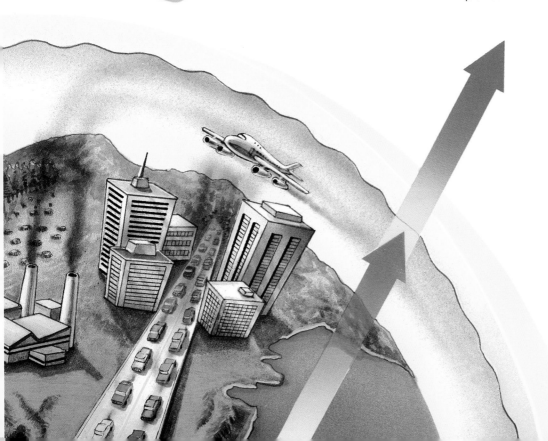

13

STOPPING GLOBAL WARMING
Controlling Carbon Dioxide

Carbon dioxide is the most difficult greenhouse gas to control because it is everywhere. It is a basic building block for everything that lives on Earth. When **fossil fuels**, such as oil and coal, are burned to run our cars or produce electricity, they react with oxygen to produce carbon dioxide. Thus, fossil fuels are a main source of carbon dioxide in the air. When people and animals breathe, they give off carbon dioxide, too.

We can't stop breathing, of course. But we must stop burning so much fossil fuel if we want to stop global warming. Scientists are working on new kinds of cars and furnaces that run on **solar power** instead of fossil fuels. Until these inventions are perfected, we can avoid wasting fossil fuels simply by driving cars less.

Opposite, top: A cement factory in Pakistan.

Opposite, bottom: Solar reflectors can be used to heat water and generate electricity.

Left: Each car on Earth produces 20 pounds (9 kg) of carbon dioxide for every gallon of gas it burns.

Cutting Back on Methane

It seems hard to believe, but cattle contribute in a big way to global warming. They produce a greenhouse gas called **methane** as they digest their food. The world has more than one billion cattle, and each animal emits about 300 quarts (285 l) of methane a day, along with its wastes!

Methane also rises up from rice paddies and other types of farming. Methane makes up about 20 percent of the gases responsible for global warming. This gas is increasing even faster than carbon dioxide, but it will be very difficult to cut back on methane. Each year, there are more people on Earth, and they need more food to eat. More cattle and crops will be raised to feed them.

Above: Our appetite for hamburgers may be contributing to the problem of global warming. The beef for burgers comes from cattle (below), which produce massive amounts of methane during digestion.

Opposite: Farmers plant rice seedlings in China.

Clearing the Air of CFCs

Another potent group of greenhouse gases is **chlorofluorocarbons** (klor-oh-FLOOR-oh-car-buns) — or CFCs, for short. They make up about 17 percent of all greenhouse gases. CFCs are chemicals used to make many familiar products, such as refrigerators and air conditioners. CFCs are also used to make foam products like egg cartons. As these products are manufactured, CFCs escape into the atmosphere, where they can trap 10,000 times more heat than carbon dioxide! To stop global warming, factories around the world need to stop using CFCs.

CFCs are the easiest greenhouse gas to get rid of. Some countries, including the United States, Canada, and Norway, have insisted that manufacturers take CFCs out of hairspray and deodorants. Scientists are also working to find safer chemicals. But many countries, such as India and China, don't want to cut back. The countries' leaders say it is too expensive to find safer chemicals. Eventually, however, they may have no choice. All CFCs may soon be banned.

Until then, we can help cut back on CFCs. We can stop using disposable foam cups and dishes. And instead of using foam pellets to protect packages when we mail them, we can use shredded newspaper, or even popcorn — without the butter, of course.

Top: Most aerosol products, such as hairspray, are no longer permitted to contain CFCs. Bottom: Many foam products like packing pellets can easily be replaced with safe, natural materials like popcorn.

Left: Manufacturers are looking at new ways to produce foam containers without using CFCs.

Below: Refrigerators wait to have their CFCs safely removed at a recycling center in England.

FACT FILE
The Mysterious Hole in the Sky

About 15 miles (24 km) above the Earth's surface, a thin sheet of **ozone** gas surrounds the planet. This ozone layer is a shield that keeps Earth from getting too much sunlight. About 10 years ago, scientists discovered a mysterious, gaping hole in the ozone layer above the South Pole. Then they discovered that the CFCs in the atmosphere were reacting with sunlight and creating a chemical that was eating away the ozone layer.

The thinning ozone layer lets more sunlight strike the Earth. This is dangerous, since too much sunlight can cause skin cancer in people. Some scientists believe that millions of people may die from skin cancer if we do not cut back on CFCs.

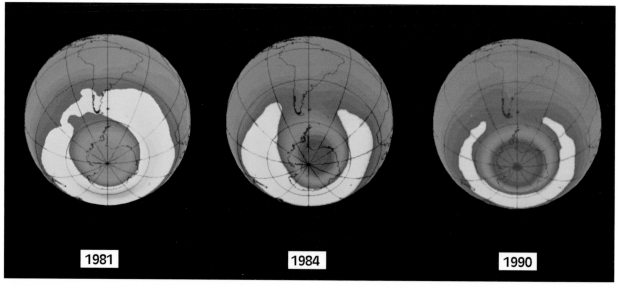

1981   1984   1990

Above: Vacationers soak up the Sun on Australia's Pacific coast.

Right: A Portuguese woman suffers from skin cancer on her lip. Some forms of skin cancer are due to overexposure to the Sun.

Opposite: Ozone is the only gas in Earth's atmosphere that can repel the Sun's ultraviolet rays. In 1981, scientists in Antarctica discovered a hole which has since become larger in this layer of gas. This illustration shows how quickly the ozone is being depleted due to CFCs rising into Earth's atmosphere.

Bringing Back the Forests

Every year, millions of acres of forests are destroyed all over the world. This is called *deforestation*. In tropical areas, forests are cut for firewood or burned to make room for farms. In other countries, forests are cut to make way for houses or to manufacture paper and lumber.

Deforestation adds to global warming in many ways. As trees grow, they store carbon in their leaves and branches. If the trees are cut and allowed to decay, the carbon they have stored reacts with oxygen and returns to the air as carbon dioxide. Burning the trees releases carbon dioxide even more quickly than cutting them down.

It is hard to get countries to stop deforestation. Poor countries use trees to grow and develop, and they say they are not the only ones causing the problem. They are right about that. The United States, for example, is one of the biggest tree consumers in the world. The average American family uses several whole trees a year in the form of paper and lumber!

Left: Ranchers have set fire to a portion of the Amazon rain forest to clear it for cattle. This land will remain productive for only a few years, and then more forest will have to be burned.

Planting more trees will not stop global warming but could help slow it down. Trees are natural air conditioners, providing cooling shade and converting carbon dioxide into oxygen. Just one acre of trees can remove more carbon dioxide from the air than the average family car produces in a whole year.

A Man Who Planted Trees

Dr. Richard St. Barbe Baker was working in Kenya, Africa, in 1922, when he became worried that too many trees in Africa were being destroyed. He formed a club with local tribesmen, who each promised to plant 10 trees every year. For the next 60 years, Dr. St. Barbe Baker helped people all over the world plant as many as 26 billion trees! The man shown in the picture above is helping to keep alive Dr. St. Barbe Baker's dream of planting and preserving Africa's trees.

Many groups throughout the world are working to stop global deforestation by planting new trees. Some groups are planting trees to help cool their cities and make them more pleasant to live in. Other groups are working to create whole new forests in areas where forests have been destroyed by nature or human carelessness.

Below: Villiagers prepare to plant trees for a future forest in Kenya.

Turning Down the Heat

Scientists are dreaming up many other creative ways to stop global warming. Maybe, they say, we can bury carbon dioxide at the bottom of the ocean, where it will not be able to trap heat. Or perhaps we can grow miles and miles of **algae** in the ocean, which will convert carbon dioxide to oxygen even faster than trees can.

These ideas are risky since no one really knows whether or not they will work. The best answer is still to cut back on the production of greenhouse gases in the first place. Many countries all over the world are getting together to talk about ways to do this. Many proposals have been made, but one thing is certain. Global warming is a worldwide problem. It can be solved only if all the countries of the world cooperate.

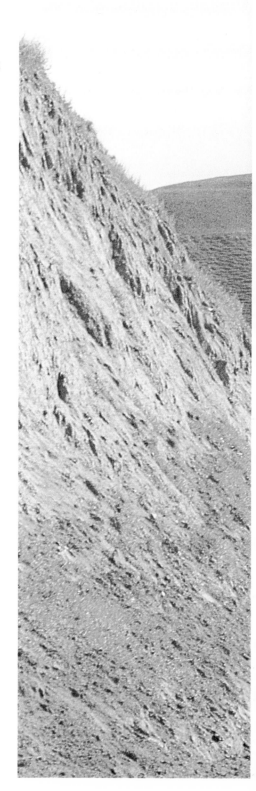

Right: People travel through the Loess Hills of Afghanistan. Because the effects of global warming are felt worldwide, solving them requires everyone's help. Unless people work together, beautiful landscapes such as this one may eventually be lost to drought or desertification.

RESEARCH ACTIVITIES

1. Make a terrarium. This miniature greenhouse is a good way to understand Earth's environment, because inside the closed glass, plants have all they need to grow. Find a large, clear glass container with a wide mouth. Fill the bottom with a layer of clean gravel, to help water drain. Cover the gravel with a layer of charcoal to keep the soil fresh. Add a few inches of potting soil on top of the charcoal. (Gardening stores have all of these materials.)

Now you are ready to plant. Dig small plants from your yard or buy them. With a pencil, poke a few holes about 1 inch (2.5 cm) deep in the soil. Place the roots of the plants in the holes and gently press the soil around them. Water the plants lightly. Cover the terrarium tightly with clear plastic and place it in a not-too-sunny location. Then it can take care of itself. The plastic holds in the warming effects of sunlight, just as Earth's atmosphere holds heat close to our planet and keeps it warm. And you won't need to water it more than once a month, because the plants use the water over and over again!

2. Find out about temperature differences. Using an outdoor thermometer, measure the temperature in a shady spot outdoors. Then place the thermometer in a sunny spot, wait a few minutes, and check the temperature again. What has happened to the temperature?

Now measure the temperature inside a car that's been parked in a sunny spot with the windows open. Then roll the windows up and leave the car for an hour. Go back to the car and test the temperature inside again. How much greater is the change in temperature when the thermometer is in the car with the windows up?

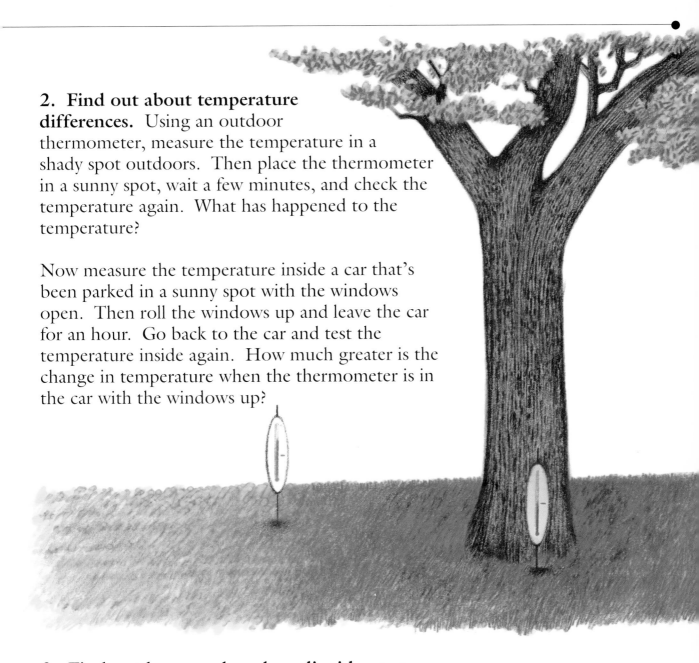

3. Find out how much carbon dioxide your class produces. Cars produce about one pound (0.5 kg) of carbon dioxide for every mile (1.6 km) driven. Ask the students in your class to count how many miles (or kilometers) they ride in the car each day. Add up the miles (or kilometers) and use these numbers to figure out how many pounds (or kilograms) of carbon dioxide your class produced by driving in one day. How many pounds (or kg) do you think the whole school produces? Your whole town?

Things You Can Do to Help

The following activities will help prevent the greenhouse effect. Try to involve your friends, family, and classmates in your conservation efforts.

1. **Cut back on fossil fuels.** Ride in the car less and walk more. Remember to turn out lights when you're not using them. Replace regular light bulbs with fluorescent bulbs, which use less energy. Make a list of other ways to burn less fuel and post the list in your classroom.

2. **Celebrate Arbor Day.** Honor the trees that help keep our planet cool. For ideas on how to do this, write to the National Arbor Day Foundation, Arbor Lodge 100, Nebraska City, NE 68410.

3. **Help plant trees.** Have your class hold a bake sale or car wash and send the money to a tree-planting program, such as Global Releaf. To find out more, write to Global Releaf, The American Forestry Association, P.O. Box 2000, Department GR2, Washington, D.C. 20013.

Places to Write for More Information

The following organizations work to halt global warming. When you write to them, be sure to tell them exactly what you want to know and include an envelope with a stamp and your address so they can write back to you.

Friends of the Trees
P.O. Box 1466
Chelan, Washington
   98816

Pollution Probe
12 Madison Avenue
Toronto, Ontario
   M5R 2S1

Trees for Life
1103 Jefferson
Wichita, Kansas
   67203

More Books to Read

Global Warming, by Laurence Pringle (Little, Brown and Company)
A Kid's Guide to How to Save the Planet, by Billy Goodman (Avon Books)
Terrariums, by John Hoke (Franklin Watts)

Glossary

algae — green, one-celled sea plants without stems, roots, or leaves.

atmosphere — the layer of gases that surrounds our planet.

carbon dioxide — a colorless, odorless gas that is formed by humans and animals breathing, the burning of plants and fossil fuels, and plant decay.

chlorofluorocarbons — gases used to create bubbles in foam packaging and as coolants in refrigerators and air conditioners.

droughts — long periods of time without rain.

fossil fuels — fuels, such as coal, oil, and natural gas, that form underground from dead plants and animals. This process takes millions of years.

glaciers — large rivers of ice that move extremely slowly.

global warming — the gradual warming of the Earth due to a buildup of heat-trapping gases in the atmosphere.

greenhouse — a glass structure in which the temperature and water are controlled for the growing of plants.

greenhouse effect — the way gases in the atmosphere hold heat close to Earth and warm it.

methane — a gas produced by matter as it decays.

oxygen — a colorless gas necessary for the survival of all plant and animal life.

ozone — a form of oxygen that acts as a shield from the Sun.

pollution — harmful or poisonous materials in the air, soil, and water.

solar power — energy that is collected from the Sun and converted into electricity.

Index

aerosol products 19
algae 26
animals 4, 6, 8, 14
atmosphere 4, 5, 12, 18

breakwater 10

cancer 20
carbon 23
carbon dioxide 12, 14, 17, 18, 23, 24, 26
cattle 17, 23
chemicals 18, 20
chlorofluorocarbons (CFCs) 18, 19, 20
climate 8
clouds 4, 5
coal 14
coastal regions 4, 6
COUNTRIES:
   Afghanistan 26;
   Australia 21;
   Bangladesh 7; Canada 18; China 17, 18;
   Ecuador 6; England 19; India 18; Kenya 24, 25; Netherlands 7; Norway 18;
   Pakistan 14; Portugal 21; Republic of the Maldives 10; United States 7, 18, 23

deforestation 23, 24
deserts 6
dinosaurs 8-9
disposable products 18
droughts 8

Earth 4, 6, 8, 12-13, 14, 20
electricity 14

factories 4, 14, 18
farmers 8
farming 6, 17, 23
flooding 6, 7, 10
foam products 18, 19
forests 22, 23, 24
fossil fuels 4, 14
furnaces 14

gases 4, 12
glaciers 8
global warming 4, 8, 10, 14, 18, 23, 24, 26
greenhouse effect 12
greenhouse gases 12, 14, 17, 18, 26
greenhouses 12, 13

ice age 8
Indian Ocean 10
islands 10

lakes 6

methane 17

North Pole 6

oceans 4, 6, 7, 26
oil 14
oxygen 12, 14, 23, 24, 26
ozone gas 20
ozone hole 20
ozone layer 5, 20

planet 4, 8, 12, 20
plants 8, 13, 17
polar ice 4, 6
pollution 12

rain forest 23
recycling center 19
rice paddies 17
Rio Guayas 6
rivers 6

sea level 6, 10
skin cancer 20, 21
solar power 14
solar rays 4, 5
solar reflectors 14
South Pole 6, 20
Sun 4, 5, 12, 21
sunlight 12, 20

temperature 8, 9, 13

waves 10